MW01264501

For Set—
who understands
that moods of the body
are the ones that matter
most. Affections,
Kelli.

Imagine Not Drowning

Poems

Kelli Allen

C&R Press
Conscious & Responsible

All Rights Reserved

Printed in the United States of America

First Edition
1 2 3 4 5 6 7 8 9

Selections of up to two pages may be reproduced without permissions. To reproduce more than two pages of any one portion of this book write to C&R Press publishers John Gosslee and Andrew Sullivan.

Cover Art by Eugenia Loli
Cover Design by Victoria Dinning

Copyright ©2016 by Kelli Allen

Library of Congress Cataloging-in-Publication Data

ISBN: 978-1-936196-68-5
LCCN: 2016956195

C&R Press
Conscious & Responsible
www.crpress.org

For special discounted bulk purchases please contact:
C&R Press sales@crpress.org

"Mankind owns four things
That are no good at sea:
Rudder, anchor, oars,
And the fear of going down."

-Antonio Machado

Kelli Allen's poems have a homespun magic that emerges from small events in nature, such as the strangeness of listening to crows make love, and they take us through dark woods and moods in ways that can remind of Robert Frost. But while Frost likes to climb toward Heaven but stay ultimately on the ground, Allen flings us into the sky with abandon, tell us to "Hurl your body /up into the rain, head bent back, throat to the clouds." This is visionary nature, lyric wildness in every cell, falling through bliss and riding wings up into the dream. In this book of parables and new fairy tales the word that keeps coming up is "home." Let these poems lift you on their wings and carry you there.

Dr. Tony Barnstone, author of *Pulp Sonnets, Beast in the Apartment, Monster Verse: Poems Human* and *Inhuman*

Kelli Allen's exquisite poems haunt me. This sensual, worshipful collection is populated by feathered creatures; ravens, crows, pelicans, soft, brown hens, and the humans who in so many ways resemble them. Hers is the natural world, its order disordered, its rituals askew. A father's death, a lover's betrayal, turn that world upside down. "We can love what's predatory/if we keep our bodies from being completely/swallowed" she writes. These beautifully crafted poems, like the heron that "swoops down from a skylight," offer a kind of salvation, taking the reader on an unforgettable journey through tragedy, grief, and redemption.

Alexis Rhone Fancher, author of *How I Lost My Virginity To Michael Cohen*, and *State of Grace: The Joshua Elegies.*

In Kelli Allen's Imagine Not Drowning, "everything begs…to be severed, to be made sweetly clean." In these poems, grief finds that clean severance, that distance tithed by loss. Though separation demands forgetfulness, the speaker resists, naming everything with memorable lyric clarity. Each poem is an archive of memory, dream, and moment. Nothing is forgotten, not the bag of mice thrown down a well, nor a nesting doll full of fathers, not even the Minotaur playing with his paper ships. Here the world and its absences are articulated, where light confirms what the dark tried to save us from--all these savage songs made sweet by distance.

Traci Brimhall, author of *Our Lady of the Ruins* and *Rookery*

In a time when American poetry is vapid and uninspiring, Kelli Allen's collection comes as a desideratum. Each poem weaves a tapestry teeming with life. Watch the way this sentence unfolds: "The paper is a wide leaf, one hundred tongues / collecting water for smoothness, gathering / my clumsy lines, knitting an image, letting / the connection turn to footsteps across // charcoal to meet your fingers now tracing / the outline of this, my intention." Each poem begs to be savored, slowly. This book is not a page-turner. And that's a good thing!

More collections of poetry are being published today than ever before. Yet, like fast food franchises, much of today's poetry leaves us malnourished and unsatisfied. I hope you have a strong appetite, because Kelli Allen's poetry is rich. She writes, "The old masters / may know all five appetites, but failing to tell / you even one means it's my turn to become a ladle / resting, steel mouth wide, in the well's water." Her reader is chewing real words. These poems are to be savored, slowly, and they will leave you nourished and satisfied.

Norman Buzz Minnick, author of *Folly* and *To Taste the Water*

Kelli Allen's Imagine Not Drowning is a collection with a strong voice with a tinge of magical realism. I loved the mythological elements and the way the poems keep me crossing or erasing those boundaries between humans and animals. Allen's amazing metaphors arise from deepest looks at the world of things, the world of living and non-living, the world of feelings. "And I came here to watch, that much is cleanly, almost certain." This is true even when the desire may be to move away from the world. There is a universal appeal here, universal exactly because it is strikingly specific and wonderfully peculiar. There is both doubt and frightening certainty in the words chosen to build the space and time for humans and creatures. As all great poetry, Allen's fresh outlook has immediate appeal but the words require work, require remembering, and revisiting.

Adnan Mahmutovic, author of *How to Fare Well* and *Stay Fair*

Charles Wright once wrote, Just give me the names for things, just give me their real names, not what we call them but what they call themselves when no one is listening. In this powerful collection of eighty muscular poems by Kelli Allen, the body bears witness to the oracular voice of the poet, conjurer and auger, naming the world, an incantation of wildness and wonder, stitching with language an ecstatic song. She writes, "We are nearing the door to the room where my ear/ presses close to the mat used sometimes for prayer,/ sometimes just for kneeling" Part invocation, part magnetic field of desire, language here is the joyful burst of play, birds as Annie Dillard once observed them, careening toward the ground at astounding speed and then sweeping up effortlessly. "We/ will hear his wings too late and the fruit just drops,/ jeweled carnage into the stream" Language is the syntactical thread and stitch of connection, like the nests found in field and wood, an architecture of love. And in this book language is the prophetic and nameless paths of migration between longing and home. The poems conjure and assemble with an authority that awes and sometimes frightens. She writes, " We walk, and I am pulling you along, a man/ in love with being afraid, with sometimes, / me." Here is the voice of a woman who knows, whose knowledge can strike fear and yet also binds. The voice inhabits the body, with its own authority and knowledge, a totem, a pillar, walking through the garden of the earth, creating matter and braiding with unbreakable ligature other bodies into relationship to itself, the lover, the father, all creatures, a knowledge that weaves beings disparate and flung into one source. This is language sustaining life.

Heather Derr-Smith, author of *The Bride Minaret* and *Tongue Screw*

I don't balk at all in my declaration that these are important poems. I feel nothing but inclined to follow Kelli Allen down these various paths/ poems of birth and decay (and birth again); poems where lichen, when lichen appears, is smothered in wildflowers. If one can imagine a world where Hughes and Plath had collaborated, where his nature poems and idyll landscapes were more colored (or "invaded") with Plath's keen ability for oblique and often shocking moments of synthesis—one will find a complex and consequential companion in Imagine Not Drowning, by Kelli Allen.

Erik Campbell, author of *The Corpse Pose*

The more I read Imagine Not Drowning the more I realize it is one of those rare literary artifacts; a completely individual and immersive world that is almost as staggering in its depth as it is in the wild collusion of influences at play. Throughout this book Allen's ear is finely attuned to the human experience, with familial relationships and love explored through a voice integrating an eclectic range of approaches, but most impressively combining mythology and nature with personal history so cohesively that it becomes impossible to dissect the threads that entwine so well in these works. In many of the poems Allen explores the moments between moments, stretching this space to breaking point and filling it with the author's lush diction. There is a confidence and a completeness to this book that I rarely find in poetry collections; Allen is not one to provide cookie-cutter answers or staged epiphanies, she is a poet who combines a post-modern understanding of confessionalism with mythology to lay the important questions at the feet of what is certain to be an exceedingly grateful readership.

Daniel Sluman, author of *The Terrible* and *Absence has a weight of its own*

Kelli Allen's Imagine Not Drowning is a collection with a strong voice with a tinge of magical realism. I loved the mythological elements and the way the poems keep me crossing or erasing those boundaries between humans and animals. Allen's amazing metaphors arise from deepest looks at the world of things, the world of living and non-living, the world of feelings. "And I came here to watch, that much is cleanly, almost certain." This is true even when the desire may be to move away from the world. There is a universal appeal here, universal exactly because it is strikingly specific and wonderfully peculiar. There is both doubt and frightening certainty in the words chosen to build the space and time for humans and creatures. As all great poetry, Allen's fresh outlook has immediate appeal but the words require work, require remembering, and revisiting.

Adnan Mahmutovic, author of *How to Fare Well* and *Stay Fair*

Imagine Not Drowning thrums with birds—beautifully, startlingly appearing in "rain-refusing jackets" to show us what songs we can sing from the human heart. These poems wind their way through fairy tale and return us to the world of elegy, where the sea and the forest shimmer with love and loss. Kelli Allen reminds us that in naming there is magic, and her poems are music boxes that play words like bells. What is said and what is left unsaid oscillate like sun and shade throughout these beautiful poems. As the speaker of "Separations for Fall, for Winter, too" says, "my tongue waits, turtle- /shelled in the mouth."

Tyler Mills, author of *Tongue Lyre*

The first poem in Kelli Allen's collection Imagine Not Drowning ends with the image of "jeweled carnage" and her book is full of a terrifying beauty that she invests in everyday scenes, fairy tales, and everywhere else her weird and wonderful imagination takes us. She explores love and loss and the places between them, "…a belated topography. Your gestures/ remind us both of the egg inside the egg inside/ the tree, of the terrible, involuntary waiting." The natural world is here, but it is the world of the "albino moose," the "tortoise in a wild woman's cellar," "feathered starfish," and "the fox breathing underwater." If you are looking for wonder in poetry, for the unexpected, for the surprising leaps a mind unfettered can make then read Kelli Allen's Imagine Not Drowning and enjoy being amazed as she tells us "…what it means to begin/ with anything, not knowing where it's going to go."

Jon Tribble, author of *Natural State*

"Sometimes the book is a swan," Kelli Allen declares, and we know she's right. In this swan of a book, poems transform like forest paths in fairy tales, as we are visited by Baba Yaga, by mysterious crows, by the lamented dead. It is a book full of curses, spells, and incantations. These poems would rend what is whole, and make whole what has been broken.

Shane Seely, author of *The Surface of the Lit World*

In a ragged world, Kelli Allen's Imagine Not Drowning is a meditation in richness. Forget scarcity, Allen's lyrical poems radiate with wild ferns, shoulders that become blackbirds, and a man loosening his bowtie near the river. In these generous, well-crafted poems, we are grounded in place and relationship. We are given the gift of images as each poem leads us where light rotates between fog. Allen's exquisite skill as a poet will make you dive in. Imagine Not Drowning is a collection that will pull you under in all the right ways.

-Kelli Russell Agodon, author of *Hourglass Museum* & *The Daily Poet: Day-By-Day Prompts For Your Writing Practice*

Kelli Allen writes in her collection Imagine Not Drowning, "There is a forest separate from the library/ and I will meet you first with books/ tight under my arm, than again with leaves/ in my hair." This is a collection where the moment overwhelms the narrative. It reminds us that life, when fully lived, isn't a story but an immersion into water without drowning, sky without falling, fire without burning, and earth without burial. In the forest of Allen's invention, there is no leaf is left unexamined.

Nicelle Davis, author of *In The Circus of You*, *Becoming Judas*, and *Circe*

Have you ever seen that toddler toy—you shake it up and peer through its clear sides, sifting through beads to spot a ring, a jewel, a coin? That's a lot like the poems in Imagine Not Drowning by Kelli Allen. This collection is completely out of the ordinary, and it's jam-packed with stuff. Every poem presents some visual image, some thing for a reader to latch onto, and, from a firebird to catch a ride on in the first poem clear through to a rope bridge to climb out on at the end, the stuff of Allen's poems is just waiting to transport a reader. The collection certainly transported me, as I read it through in one long sitting, taking plenty of time between poems to linger amid the artifacts.

Karen Craigo, author of *No More Milk* (Sundress, 2016) and *Passing Through Humansville* (ELJ, forthcoming 2017)

What a curious bestiary, Imagine Not Drowning, the "black ducks / tucked in rain-refusing jackets," the sparrows "agitated / and waiting." Kelli Allen writes poems with a "determined appetite"—poems mythic, allusive, and just out of reach. "I want this experience to be unpolluted," she writes, knowing full well that experience is pollution. "There is a grackle who reminds us that it is not yet / too late." But of course it is. And yet. In Allen's own words: "These outstretched songs are fierce."

Randall Mann, author of *Straight Razor*

Kelli Allen's Imagine Not Drowning it is not an unreal or dream world, but a fantastical alternate reality that exists just under the skin of the quotidian. Kelli Allen says, "We live everyday/ with a child we do not know." That is the being that lives within the pressure suit of the human body. Kelli Allen takes us deep to strange things that are eerily familiar, and she does so with a language that is strikingly fresh and musical. "It's the accidental gifts that we trip over/on our way around the desert, the cacti blooming/hard. We endure rot because the music ants play/marks the first song we hear last."

Rustin Larson, author of *Crazy Star, The Wine-Dark House, Bum Cantos*, and *The Philosopher Savant*

Imagine Ophelia floating from the pebbled riverbank, singing in her skirts and flowers. Where does she go from here? Imagine her not drowning. Imagine Ophelia "…checking / not for pulse but for birds, lilies, trapped…," collecting "wrists / with [her] tongue," and ultimately writing "a lifelong sentence toward home"—a home she may never see. This is Kelli Allen's praise song and elegy, a sumptuous treasure box brimming with Sharon Olds' intimacy and the knotted, slippery syntax of Carl Phillips. "Sometimes the book is a swan," writes Allen. Indeed, though with her as our guide, we will just as eagerly follow "the jeweled carnage into the stream."

Sandra Marchetti, author of *Confluence* and *Sight Lines*

Kelli Allen's words soar, seem as carefully chosen as the silences, what her speaker will not say. Her images are surprising and true, and I find myself smiling with admiration as I read her work. Moreover, Imagine Not Drowning is a sideways look at love and longing and hope, tender and fragile emotions anchored to this world by the music of language.

Mary Troy, author of *Swimming on Highway N*

Imagine Not Drowning

CONTENTS

5~ Becoming a Woman of the Brook, Shade, and Moss

6~ Market Day in Someone Else's City

7~ Feeding Birds, or, rather, Some Magic

8~ Folding the Invitation to Your Wedding

9~ The Rooster's Daydream

10~ Late Afternoon in the Tall Grass

11~ Here Are Instructions for Removing the Scissors

12~ Eventually, we go inside

13~ Wishing Adeline and the Shooting Stars

14~ If Fairy Tales in Fall

15~ Eleven Years, Abandon Another Day

16~ Sorrow's Argument

17~We, As Other People

18~ What of Birds

19~ Trebuchet

20~ Aphasia

21~ When He Leaves

22~ How Much Tenderness, When We Consider How to Leave

23~ Of Five Fears: Three of them light.

25~ Separations for Fall, for Winter, too

26~ Edging Our Wall, Untying

27~ Deciding Against Marriage

28~ Some Animals

29~ Stopping to Retrieve What Might Be Lost in the Brush, Quiet

30~ Ghosting

31~North Fork

32~ Conversation Under Sun In Summer, Late

33~ What Can We Do To Be Away From the World?

34~ Hushing, like an awl through leather

35~ Walking through the morning

36~ Reformation

37~ Riding the borrowed cow back home

38~This Is How You Ask Me How To Pray

39~ Invitations Toward Autumn
40~ When this is not about sentiment
41~ Blood on your toes and predators at your heels
42~ Here Is The Blurry Mark, The Sometimes Love Letter
43~ Some Call This Self Defense
44~ The Night Is Designed To Save Us
45~ When We Argue About Unraveling Glass
46~ Tart Fruit, How Best to Serve A Mouth
47~ Between Your Hand and Some Answer
48~ Sometimes, as we move closer to Autumn
50~ This is how I answer goodnight
51~ Philosophy Tramples Everything , No Apologies
52~ This is the part where we don't say "love"
53~ We name the totems with every morning
54~ Still talking about endings
55~ Imagine Not Drowning
56~ Every Day We Devour the One Before
57~ It's Only A Weapon When You Hold Your Breath
58~ The Prettiness Is Up-Close
59~ You Say Disappear And I Say Not Yet
60~ There Are Ships Closer If You Let Them
61~ There is Enough Morning to Cleave the Skull From the Coral
62~ It's Only Running If You Refuse To Get Lost
63~ Bravery, you said, is not what it used to be
64~ Each of us a temple, a banquet lain over the cape
65~ There are shortcuts for burning the world
66~ Unbreakable hour after hour
67~ We replace the knives when the light appears
68~ Walking the lover past starlings' nests
69~ This is the center of disappear
70~ We come in anyway
71~ Quills are for the stories that stay written
72~ We make nothing from instinct
73~ The animal we love wags its tail even in the new dark
74~ How Far We Dive Is Only A Distraction
75~ If your chest to my spine is not quite enough
76~ Seduction is the Lightening from this Season into Next
77~ Starch Coming First, Filling Hands Before Mouths Met Brine
78~ Seeing a Teeth Mother Mask, Together, On A Friday Afternoon
79~ If the door notices you watching, it's only polite to look away

Becoming a Woman of the Brook, Shade, and Moss

What if my body fell through bliss,
caught its last small toe on some hook
in descent? How, then, will we name
wherever is left, is aswirl, skull and clavicle
force-sculpted, at last, having roughly
fallen together to rest (wait) at the bottom
of my well, and certainly yours?

You tell me it's easy to pretend Ivan
will make room on his flaming bird's back,
when we are ready to be lifted, however restlessly,
away from woods, sea, maybe our bed suddenly
too small, knotted. You promise the feather's heat
will be worth the untying, the recognition
of this loss exchanged for riding away,
Yaga's hut distant, withering. Despite warnings,
there are only three ways to bury shame.

Before long we're asleep, mats spread over pebbles,
pillows wilted, and the beetle arrives with our keys
tucked in mandibles, tusks. The next day might
not come and no fortune hunter can reclaim
what was lost in the tucking in, folding under,
of these blankets too cool under our chins. We
will hear his wings too late and the fruit just drops,
jeweled carnage into the stream.

Market Day in Someone Else's City

Some towns are the wing bones we crush
in our hands. Every streets' turn signifies
what is most hollow in the snap. Yet,
we return again as weasels emerging
from the rough barn, paws and teeth
ahold of the last map, rich cake crumbs
still falling from the scrolls' edges.

Leaving means we close the garden house
door, maybe too late, and who then will escort
the bride, her two blessed boys, and some
prince to the hall erected as center, as castle?

It's no longer enough to be the merchant
when rain refuses an audience and the procession
could stop, and there are no dances to sell,
no poppies left in our baskets, the ground dust,
too rough for this white calf, our only meal,
to lead the way ever, closer, nearly home.

Feeding Birds, or, rather, Some Magic

They grow overnight, these black ducks
tucked in rain-refusing jackets, their feathers
blooming outward, once turning inward, sharp,
a pendulum humming a remembered remainder
of simple dreams—the prize for another night
spent still on water, orders for feeding forgotten.

Yours is the smallest bird, the once braced along-
side a periphery of awake and not quite. Yours
is the association of warm under the down,
nothing tainted or hardened by an afternoon
guessing which of your wings will prove
greenest when the sun agrees to provide
just enough light to make all of this more,
never less, than water from your dream to mine.

Folding the Invitation to Your Wedding

There is a plow waiting near my broken flashlight. Both
promise a variation of warmth, perhaps warmth though
what I can expect to carry by pushing under, giving root,
perhaps by some illumination not yet anchored enough
for closeness here, this page asking for response, for
a bond of sorts. What can I ask of you? You who lets a foot
stay tucked under warm sand, hands in pockets, coarse
hair falling ever over one cheek or the other? The curve
of you a fleshy question mark near such open waters.

Why this snuggle into writing when shown the useless
tool and the cylinder all broken plastic and glass? Objects
meant to signify desire for reciprocity become, instead,
talismans for clumsy loss, for wanting more, always more,
than I am ready to let bare in the dirt. It's pale, when it touches
my skin, this god-hand of distance, this god-touch of absence.

The Rooster's Daydream

My father was a swelling over
the soft brown hen, his beak punctuating
her neck, irrigating her dreams
of chicks drying their fluff near rocks
pebbling the curve around her stream.

Their bodies moved in an unfurling, both
trying not to be harsh with the other
in this sun, in the open dirt where fences
dotted a periphery. Theirs was a blooming,
however sudden, warped by cats narrowing
eyes, snakes uncoiling in the heat and noise.

His adoration was quick in the way
that fingers are fast when dipping
into a honeycomb, exploring the beehive
just long enough to gather sweetness
in secret. When the trees ripen,
I remember first the gathering of sound,
ghosted couplings and feathers
everywhere under their rough claws.

When the petals fall waxy in pools,
I imagine my father retrieving
his posture, letting the hen, my mother, curl away
from his wing and neither he nor she
can possibly notice the waiting ax, its nest
a richly ringed post, old-berry red, alert.

My body is the population left
in this dreaming. My breast a constellation
of hollow quill and down resting on one
blossom after another, their pink hearts tiny
boats carrying me as an eyelet snapping,
finally, against perfect silver metal. My head
bent on the way to receiving my crown.

Late Afternoon in Tall Grass

Mice rest their knees against softening dirt
and we turn further away from the east.

When I sat upon my horse, waiting
for you to come outside, I saw the henhouse shades
move twice with breeze we talked about all morning—
how it forces our halls to smell like cinnamon until night.

There are exhausted wrens dotting the ground near these hooves.
I have not seen a grub for miles. One thin-breasted bird
shifts her leg and everything near golden tufts into the air, a circus.

We used to rush around, with these bodies set tight as jaws
and missed the dandelion boats skimming our legs as we ran,
hurried for the shore that somehow never moved as far away
from our sobriety as we from its drunken lap and swirl over sand.

When you come, there might still be stones in my pocket, bread
packed neatly in the saddle, a balance cast while pretending
the path to some castle must be here, marked by the angleworms
drying flat near old rainwater in our field.

Here Are Instructions for Removing the Scissors

Take the bribe offered and just plunge your entire
arm, full past the twist of elbow, into the cool muck.

Take this moment as opening of determined appetite—
the blades are yours once pulled into the grass. Yours.

Take whatever weird laughter you hear behind your shoulder
as balm, a resolve for how far you can open, can exhale, and search.

Take slippery weeds, darkening further down, lightening as they snake
up your wrist into the fading day, as a message—everything feeds, waits.

Take dense mud around your fingers and pull tightly the looped handle
as you dislodge the entirety of silver from this reeking, shallow pond.

Take every opportunity to own and wield the weapons for cutting, as
every-
thing begs, at some sharp moment, to be severed, to be made sweetly
clean.

Eventually, we go inside.

You stack the stones as rabbits
mounted one atop the other, this field
in blue light, moss peppered with heather,
sometimes wild ferns, licking behind
your ankles as you work.

When we stepped into this opening, flanked
by mirroring puddles, and the sand hill
maze sat far behind, we knew
the thickest part of finding our way
back would come long after
a conversation, punctuated as it would be
with silences, and shuffling our feet
in rough, complicated circles—you
building pillars instead of gathering my fingers
in yours, reassuring, communing, and me,
watching your hands fill only with stones.

Even after I let my sweater fall open, then drop
to whorl into an angora pool in the thistle-pocked
clover against your boot, you would not stop
building, higher and more delicately balanced,
with those rocks, filigree against this darkening sky.
I breathed touch me and the words met with only air,
the spell cast becoming little other than pennies
left on the path, the one we marked, some time
ago, in chalked letters, as this way, home.

Wishing Adeline and the Shooting Stars

Sometimes the book is a swan. Moments will pass and pages will curl up and away and the lines are lost for an hour as words find succor in a pond close to our window. This is not a story about goodbye. We may not know how to lurch from this world into the next, but we understand the impulse to keep our softest feathers just above water, our tails flinching toward something like sky, something like sheets billowing above us. I have neglected to tell you that not once in my whole life have I left the slipper on the stairs. Perhaps this is a story about leaving, but the kind that you and I never do, our attention as rabbits nuzzling the leash.

I made a wish, which is risky and makes you captive to the telling, but when the dandelion pop decided to loose every seed at once, what choice did I have? So many limbs are invisible in their last blossomings, even when scattering after my own pinkish tongue begs the field, the bigger flower, to wait, wait.

When we claim it, the book comes home and the story is finally about closing tight, a wishing won. I am steadfast, unruly in my quiet, and my eyes shut twice when I remember you, too, taste the busy stems as they fall beneath us.

If Fairy Tales in Fall

It isn't so much that the leaves are dizzy as it is they are lodged in confusion, the same variety that persuades us to jump when the waters are on the rise. We say, "look" as our feet reappear after tumbling over our shoulders on the way down, we tremble and spill over. The repair work is universal as the rake scratches our sides.

I contain so much thinning, yet lushness is my fresco when I stop at the bottom of the well, climb back into the bucket and yell up "It matters! It matters!" until only the rope tail hangs near the stone rim. Nothing whorls up in a shock the way a name does, when its ours, all peacock and hiss, all vowel and cinnamon.

You have been told how to cut back the trestle, to light the lamp and fold your hands. This way, we are advocates together for a splayed phrase and retelling. The only stories we can give back are ones considerate of the moss digesting the ledge.

Eleven Years, Abandon Another Day

You still push the envelopes through the iron rails
onto grass seldom cut, leaving the bright papers to wait
tiny bird-light, for a possible wind to carry them closer
to her front door. It is disaster to push against the cold
and watch you. Your gesture is a song and my stale brow
is the bag of mice our father threw down the well, punctuating
our final summer in his home with something easier for him
to say than forget it all.

She left her own note, a simple paragraph framed
by pink and yellow tea roses. I read the words to you
because our father hunched into his own curl of disbelief
and remained round in some residue of voice that leaned
more into silence than rough cries, which we heard only once,
at night. Somehow this matters in the way that cats carry
the nearly dead to their kittens as an offering, yes, and a command.

We listen on the way back to my house, where I teach you again
how not to vanish, for bells from her church to ring the hour,
exactly seven tones, all even. This has become home despite
his filling with smoke, hers with simple, dark corners, yours,
always tethered, twin orphans in a terminal made of sand, to mine.

Sorrow's Argument

On the day before we learn to distrust it, grief is welcome.
It soaks us with heavy wet gratitude in being able to feel
anything at all. We take grief down into our throats and hold
it thick just above our bellies. The not quite fullness reminds us
of the way back up and through, past our lips, is breath and, eventually,
song. There are four words for this: *waiting, resistance, sigh, alchemy.*

The day it arrives fully announced and inconsiderate of our day-
dreams, we pretend its calls are to others and leave the door
soundly shut. Grief, when eaten too quickly, burns the stomach
bright with holes meant for falling through, inside out, and no well
equals the pitch and pull we glimpse only after we tumble over
the edge. There are four words for this: *bags, root, turning, final.*

In the days after, grief is christened soft sorrow, seeming as white
snow piling all afternoon while children sleep. Sorrow is a mysterious
thief taking wasps carrying our grief into an unknown, distant summer.
We should be thankful and blink, laugh. They are neighbors, grief and
sorrow, as their trickery is our acceptance of blindness, our desire for
something sweet. There are four words for this: *attachment, underbelly,
heft, charity.*

We, As Other People

We've been very happy in the small open area
we named alter. When we lay down
it is a fragile offering, ellipses of arms,
galaxies of fox-light hairs, moving,
a division between tremble and bristle.

This is what other people do in the dark.

Sometimes, they let light in and the scene
shifts. There are occasions for fire,
kindling as mirror, candles, too, for them-
bodies without growing dis-ease, anchored
to luck, devouring wishless time. Others
are fragrant with each other, bits
of raspberries wait on their tongues.

Not us. Ours is the thumbtack mapping
where in my body the image darkens, where
under inverted triangles of breast meeting breast
the roundness grows cloudy. We live, devour
by recent scans, which we will continue
to hang here, this museum of us, until alter
becomes shrine, becomes definition for a new
lover. Here were other people, who were us, before you.

What of Birds?

We credit the feather's shape for their momentum, but our own battered skin flutters unseen, toward errors of unknowing. We are spoons turned against capturing wetness, slick curves refusing to bow inward. To communicate softness in avigation, we must forget impulses tentative, and just, as they do, these birds, dive behind currents. This is saying hide; this is saying it's too much to care. When I ask you if there has been a difference in one thousand years of eyes trained upward, forced through certain jealously, into awe, I expect an answer laced through with an erudition enough to make me properly jealous. It is too easy to accept the son overtaking the father, a breeze breathing the young higher, the aged remaining an immobile windmill by the barn. This is my response to your response, leaving us no closer to reprieve. We might never know how to explain what hurts us as we travel through one alliance after another, no closer to our own waxless flight.

Trebuchet

It is easy to hide
one father inside
of another, as you have,
my father, so many of you
tucked tight, as nesting
dolls without seams.
As the painted wooden set
you brought back to me
from Holland, each miniature face
smaller than the one before.

Those dolls made sense,
in their nestling logic, though
sense is a weak gray raven
to a small girl.

Now, when you cannot speak
through any of your mouths
and I have learned to lean
against your shoulder
as you lean into mine
for the first time, the dolls
will no longer open. Whatever passes
for secret belongs to them, paint
cracked only slightly, seams tight, sticking.

I think of lambs, sometimes
covered in thick zebra's stripes,
embossed to the touch,
and their new bodies
become one of you.

Aphasia

You know the way it broke
loose, the brick, from inside
our second house, a moment before
we decided on breakfast. You said

> *I put both hands in the space*
> *where the mortar took rot, both hands. Still*
> *the clay won't take, I cannot force a brick.*

Today is like that, with me watching your thick fingers
paused as cups in the air, sensing the way your hands gathered
the red chips and dust from our floor. Now, both hands
wait for something else to fall into them. It isn't just
your face, wet from internal rain, telling me to surrender.

When I said Dad and you could not turn to meet my voice,
when only those hands lifted out and up, palms too dry,
could I remember that none of us live in a room, that our walls,
no matter how they pinch and pioneer our lessons, contain
so little of what we often meant to say. Really say.

When He Leaves

The stamp on the back of her hand has faded
the same way a favorite tree stump stays
against some remembrance of childhood
we no longer attempt to name.

When the ink was fresh, it was a simple possibility
of a bluish shark, lines a-fuzz, teeth obscured,
the cartoon bubbliness of a shape made to exorcise
fear, to produce momentary joy. For her,
the image marked time spent with her father
after one morning chasing mottled geese, grey
as January, through the only park she knows
this well. She asks for balloons, a bouquet to affirm
light, and she is gifted both the blossoms of thin color
and a single pale stamp from a vendor charmed
into stooping low and adoring her pale, pale skin.

So, it tastes like something, this moment before
I let the words leave my mouth. Not quite
bitter, or pungent the way she and I both love
dark olives, pits intact, hard reminders. No,
it tastes like softness, as when bread goes beyond
staleness into the waiting for greens and acceptance
of being covered, lost completely, transformed.

How Much Tenderness, When We Consider How To Leave

We said it would be dry by morning, and so left
your name, wet, on the doorframe. It was simple,
to leave this bodily inked artifact of you as something
of a warning against entrance: Come in, please, but know
everything died within and left signatures without.

The burial was more complicated. We sat you between us
on the long bench just inside the funeral parlor, admiring
the latticework of brass and wood, which served as crown
molding in this small room. I whispered, just like Alice
in the Queen's hall, and waited, looking down at the cylinder
wherein you, something of you, rested all dust and what must seem
like so many broken black sand shells to the fire keeper
who placed you first in the flames, and then, here, in this silver
capsule. I say between us, but there was really only me, if we count
presence as more than breath and completely still hands in a lap.

Interment is a misleading word. We can never blanket enough dirt
to hide what is missing. If I could have cut my heart into enough
pieces to feed you, I would have done so at least twice. Now,
I take a photograph of the earth being piled over this ringed swatch
of indentation in the ground. The image will hang loose, near
your name dried blackish against wood, an artifact to mark
every time I will pretend to knock, enter anyway, the one space
never really my home. Someone else offers the morning prayer.

Of Five Fears: Three of them *light*.

It refuses to fall from the sky, bloated
arrogance of brightness, a round bird

preening mid-air, whether we watch, or not.
And I came here to watch, that much
is cleanly, almost certain.

Nothing moves with that kind of light
forcing reflections where there should be
only darkening shadows. I am already angry

to have written shadows, light, darkening. Anger
is a shunt difficult to remove, tissues
growing around, forming something
of a structure, again, bulked against

light. Letting it in, this light, again
seeing the word here, means imaging

the bird has won-over actually allowing
the self to see a wing, feel
a ripped feather, watch the feeding.

Separations for Fall, for Winter, too

What's unlikely is this rain. Even
the sparrows are agitated
and waiting. But I am contacting
you not for some contract to be signed,
finally. Rather, I want us to hurry
across and ripen the letters for evidence
of closing. We have lodged
complaints before and each skims
the pond quick, a rehearsal we perform
in fog. What is likely is assumed distance.

We are not the same small animals
curled against blurred margins
and dropped pebbles. Our hands let
go their thefts months ago. I can hardly
remember accumulations. This is
to convey regret, maybe desire,
too, as my tongue waits, turtle-
shelled in the mouth.

Edging Our Wall, Untying

There is pressure between my hand and the reaching. We ask
longing to become a city for us, but what do we say
when the windows blow inward instead of out
and the streets flood again and again? If I am the length
of this want, and you are the width of some container
as we build up and out, how can we hope to plant grass
near the temple which will be, of course, the center of it all?

I have a bag attached to one wrist and blueprints tight
in a scroll attached to the other. Leaving either on the road
means that we are finished. There are tourists afoot and we
are drenched in something like snow. This may be a diagnosis
I am offering. It may be a solution for the obvious anxiety
of bending our faces down, teeth spaced
to let the wind come in, come in.

Deciding Against Marriage

It is a jeweled evening and everything,
everywhere is mechanical bliss. We have
forgotten migration and these cogs
stand-in for feathered movements.

The oils are as rich as ever, even
though they coat copper and water
wicks its way off other wings.

Ours is an automated afterglow. The release
comes in the rewind, the start-again of wheels
crafted in what might have been our back-
yard had we waded deep enough in the muck to ask.

Some Animals

There is a patterned crosshatch in the armor
and no amount of rubbing lessens its impact.

Distraction is the handmaiden of complacency,
or some such thing. I am waiting for a trick

of light to let me shout "what a kingdom!" and go away,
heels clicking onetwo onetwo on the marble leading out.

I want this experience to be unpolluted. I want the end
to be a trajectory of my own making. Nothing upsets

contentment quicker than intentionally disturbed metal.
Where is the glimmer, the Alexandrian hangman of glory

cast against steel? Sometimes the only salvation
is in the heron that swoops down from a skylight

we did not even notice to spread wing and waters
over the arch of a shield, of a blade.

Stopping to Retrieve What Might Be Lost in the Brush, Quiet

Late afternoon, Tuesday, I have gathered
sixteen leaves into four stacks, and a dog
wanders closer to my clean patch of dirt

and moss, and this book of symbols
is open to the first page on interlocking circles,
and four hours of collecting hues
through a borrowed lens feels too brief,

and this final autumn egg sits askew, broken
open, sticky, not drying fast enough, and the dog
is coming too close, coming soon, and some winter

begins collecting itself near hatchings left
to wander into this too early night, and I stand,
bend at the waist, and look inside.

Ghosting

Who points the way, holds out a gloved hand
with a single, simple sign stating This way?
What book officially begs us to give attention
to a list of rules which includes You may only ask
one question of the steward? What if the answer
to both queries has been carved in shallow print
into soap stone ever nearing the shoreline's
inevitable lick and curl? We should admit
there is sense in answers near wetness. Swallowing
is its own sign—a reflex won at birth, repeated
with every phrase, every taken pleasure.

I think of this as ghosting. What came before
certainly does not wish for us to forget
and so offers a seeding of questions, which we embrace
without intention, and this I call, not paranoia,
rather knowing-lust. That radiance we suspect
has been threaded into our every lysosome, namelessly,
unearned, ours as a right of carrying cells upon
cells until we think we might be whole, is never
really new and so we keep vigil for signifiers.

North Fork

The sign warns of undercurrent
and as you read the words aloud, against
my ear, against this water rushing hard, elevating
minute hairs with breath, yours, I intend to listen, can't,
and so exhale sharp, marking the new distance with mint,
with steam, where a warning might have been.

Earlier today, when you gentle rough took my wrist with your fingers
tight
and quick whispered look and hush and I saw, as you did, the small doe,
close enough to stroke with the fingers not now laced through yours,
and you told me that deer are intention beyond sight, hunger, nothing,
you say,
everything, I promise, special. Her underbelly teems, fur
a swirling surface, a warm agate moving, somehow, above
tall grass browning too soon.

Watching you watch her I close my eyes for maybe two breaths
and let you become the buck quickening in his circle to meet her,
the buck that somehow holds me in his periphery the way I expect
to be pressed from finger pads to palm when your outstretched arm
collects my shoulder, too briefly, too much saying not yet.

And now, when rocks lodge between metal slats under your boots
and when your hands rest still in their pockets, I can hear
each soft plunk as first one stone, then another, loosens
from iron into wet. This is to say I am sorry
to have let your arms tuck close to your chest instead
of circling, as moments before they begged, my waist.

Conversation Under Sun In Summer, Late

The ear has its own mood, wants
to succeed, wants to know
more than the curve and bell
of itself. The ear finds water rushing,
confesses mistakes easily, begs
to be cupped against dampness,
against translations in the upper register.

We speculate that there is a noble problem
when the ear resists our distinctions, lumps
us together in a singular song, leaves us
to our own arguments, even though our knees touch
once and my fingers find again, too quick, your shoulder.
We are over-flown with sounds marked less
by contrast than by interference. I hear your lips
against the cup and wonder where.... when.

Perhaps the teacher has taught her student
to listen through the mouth. There is safety
in the simple shape of each vowel. Leave
the ear to a shade of enthusiastic ripeness
gathered when the head is pushed closely, tilted
to catch a dress's hem sighing up from a damp thigh.

We are nearing the door to the room where my ear
presses close to the mat used sometimes for prayer,
sometimes just for kneeling.

What Can We Do To Be Away From the World?

We think we might go north, the way the stamen puffs firm
against mid-day breeze. It's an old silence that gives us pause,
makes us bend our spines back into the pillows, you reaching
up to push the window a crack higher, the length of your arm
dangerous in its pale, in my desire to trace the elbow's bend
once with my tongue tipped hard.

The way you worry is an easy country compared to just how much
I keep hidden, the weight of hiding becoming its own
language when we meet, later in the day, the week, as strangers.

Those maps for whatever comes in the pretending night
when you have climbed above me, slow pushing, being taken
inward, are peeling quickly from the brick and I catch your eye,
just once, widening as you recognize that when paper meets ground,
we will have nothing left to plan, to explain, to wish.

Hushing, like an awl through leather

First, the body is bent. And we
barely speak into the maw
of the potbellied stove
as we feed logs tighter
into such fullness.

Someone I knew once
hummed each movement
from that song you love
and now, while you arch
your back into stretch, bones
a whimper through this too cool night,
I want nothing more
than to slither soft behind
and collect your wrists
with my tongue while you tell me
what it is to crave a proper scratch
behind hairy ears. We might meet
again, later

in leanings against that old church,
its bell weighted by your stories, not mine,
and I will tell you, then, ash still
under my boot, why I asked you
to come inside.

Walking through the morning

You may have slept all night and we walk
together past the horses, who are out early
on this Sunday and their necks bending
down becomes the prologue for this: I saw you carry
your boots, cradle them as oysters plucked too soon
from cool brine. The mud, you told me later, came
from the river, undersides of oak and willow pocking
leather. It does not matter where you decide to rest
the objects you value. It matters even less
how such labor is as perishable as the apple
rolling by your bare feet.

The mares don't see us as we see ourselves, as I
look at you and say "Dear one. Never mind.
you were already come and gone. I made the bed
up tight. The lights are on. They're still on."

Reformation

I drew a woman's ankles to make room for the guest
of this want, the bony sharpness of its presence.

The paper is a wide leaf, one hundred tongues
collecting water for smoothness, gathering
my clumsy lines, knitting an image, letting
the connection turn to footsteps across

charcoal to meet your fingers now tracing
the outline of this, my intention. A bell slung low
over the thousand doors on a map made
from honey, stingers drying in the new thickness,
rings twice when you bring the page to your mouth,
inhale. Do not waste the evening waiting

for me to return. I am growing the tiny, busy
grape of your heart in the milk and brine
poured over this winter ground. Every night
is a lifelong sentence about home.

Riding the borrowed cow back home

Do not expect me to court forgetfulness, not now
after I have allowed you to hug my grief under
more than a willow. You slept all night

with every window closed and this perishable
body memorized the recklessness
of your stillness. We confessed so little,
but I found this poem in the morning,
and retrieved what pleasures
someone else might have wasted.

I am admitting that there are ragged
words for feeding. Everywhere we long
for some madness agreed upon
when we lost our fathers, when we thanked
night for coming back home, and remembered
too soon our friendship with ruined things.

This Is How You Ask Me To Pray

Now we might understand the crow
when she kisses her beak to his,

the lover, the sleeper tired of us,
but not the expanse above

our dusty spaces. How many times
have we walked beneath the tree

and mistaken the low cries
for some weird wind? We know

our haunches resist the dirt
when we lean back against

the old church wall in its yard, a plow
and apple cart set as stage pieces

to catch the feathers ruffled hard
and down from bird tongues

too tangled to believe. When you stop
us both under the last branch, this October

day, we do not join hands, nor fall
asleep, no hooves tampering

leafy beds, or palms covering knees
when the kneel becomes inevitable.

Invitations Toward Autumn

There is a forest separate from the library
and I will meet you first with books
tight under my arm, then again with leaves
in my hair. We have both stood at the edge
of this town, asking whatever passes for god
to listen, just this once, while we tell a story.

I have straightened the vases in my house, arranged
them in rows to collect the daisies I expect
you to bring, plucked fresh as they were
from the road garden, not yours, not mine.

Sometimes the window is open
at just the right moment and we look through
glass quickly, pulling the outside fire as a parachute
collapsed, inward, to settle around this table,
laden as it is with tiny bees, my notebooks,
your palms, upward turned, catching first
my elbow as I rise to push wider the panes,
letting the first storms come in, rounding
our shoulders, this suddenness.

When this is not about sentiment

In the long mornings, our bellies
crouch between fingers bending
toward thumbs in the first pinch
of skin to see if the other
is awake, is still a shining fish
in a dream where scales
leave dark pits in the mud.

We know where our feet go,
cool wounds nestled in blankets,
betraying nothing of where
and how they walked along the river.

Shoulders never fit anywhere,
so we press them down as white
birds into just new snow, turn
closer toward, inward, and before
you ask if I do, I bite your lip yes
and move a thousand years past
your cheekbones in this too early light.

Blood on your toes and predators at your heels

We carry our daily dissections down
into the gut, where the words
vanish, their own bodies speechless.

The fact is, love never comes
on purpose. You wait for intention
and the underworld opens delicate
and the heat is less, and more,
than you expected, like the one
sticky thorn we miss when wandering
too close to the old barn's side door.

The quiet is a levitation, when the skin
opens and we all hush to watch
first one muscle ripple then the next.
We are lichen-tough in our refusal
to look away. When we are all the way

under and ask *am I not deserving?*
this is the moment we know who
visits from all four corners
the way the dead know the pretense
in their blinding. What is left

are the lips pursed round to whistle
the song made sweet by distance.

If I Write A Narrative Poem It Will Be This One

He orders tomato juice and I think, of course,
blood, and wonder at the sense memory, how
quickly it comes and from where. I ask, too,
if the thighs meeting under the table might
promise another hunger, but not like last
night, where ineffectual time had nothing
on the half bottle of cheap whisky
collecting in our chests, pulling our hand
strings closer to the other's body.

I won't admit remembering the stones
under his shoes as we ascended the hill
below that ugly church. Light gifted
from one of two streetlamps did not entirely
collect as champagne bubbles along the rough
line of his jaw. When fingering a gathered
bit of shale, now, in morning openness,
I am suddenly the widow on fire. I have become

the woman, he says, he might have wanted
before falling one too many times
from the roofs like those in the photo
he folds again as surrender, sometimes
as drowning, and he drinks the red thick
into his belly, where last night, my mouth
said an autumnal, honeysuckle prayer.

Some Call This Self Defense

It's corrosive, the mirror, some face
dying in snow thick enough to bury
luggage and your lover, both. So, what
does looking publish about the mysterious
ticket that is you, a wound, a drink, a body?

Understand that it is painful work to stitch
inertia and hours and talent into skin
vulgarized by what you think you inherit.
Come money, come time, come hands, all

unremitting even when you lower your arms,
clear the steam from glass, whisper hurry
backwards into the rising, rising fog.

The Night Is Designed To Save Us

A carnival in daylight is an unfinished beast.
This might be where the prayers go,
the ones we cast upward in the dark, too thick
for brightness, too much shame for stories
told in sunlit patches of dirt, moss.

The foxes are growing up and this, too,
is a resurrection. I have been both
the blue jay and his breakfast waiting
under leaves. I am not running to the brook.
I am easing toward its bank, tail aflame.

When the tents house the sleeping freaks
and I am dressed for your wedding, where
will I lay soft this net for collecting fish
as they jump into their terrible distances,
closer to the bear's maw than the gifted basket?

My talent is to live through the morning
from thaw to sobriety to what you called
stardust. In the end, we improvise. In the end
we keep one foot on either side of center ring.

When We Argue About Unraveling Glass

You want panic? Let me show you
the Maypole dance constructed
underwater, where the tardigrades
have resorted to glass instead
of shotgun flames, the kind you love
in old movies, in the older country.

These outstretched songs are fierce,
but not enough for you, singer, rock
collector too good for lava stone, too
whole for my cracked humming.

Show me how you risk blisters
placing that hand by this fire. I won't
believe you unless I, too, am falling
through mud to get closer to coal
and the King's retainer. So, tell me

the story one more time. Remind me
that one year is too long for a finch
but just an eyelash bat for a water bear.

Somewhere in your body you swallowed
down both the instrument and the surplus
and now the cherub flies fast with both
our crowns and you just stretch and stretch.

Tart Fruit, How Best to Serve A Mouth

Let's pretend you are hungry
and I have a created a rubric
for eating. You are exhausted
and the berry stain spreads
from a finger tip trailing upward.

I have kept track of your faith,
this being a prayer, too, such opening
of first one mouth, then the other.

The truth is, it would be easier to practice
slow extinguishment if you close your lips,
heroic trust some frontier you recognize.

Let me wriggle apart those fleshy doors,
intricate lines waiting for cream as soon
as garden light, even long, long after sun
made sure to leave you cold. You wear

that want as a teacher bent on showing
her student just who started the fire
that burnt the books, and every horse,
like pastry ash into the oven's heavy ground.

Between Your Hand and Some Answer

There was ice in the river last night, floes blue
in a double blossom against current, under
hanging willow branches. I am in love

with this gathering and when you looked
at your hand in its accidental brush near
my shoulder, I remembered first to tell you
about the frozen crowning, the way ice became,
for me, a world of praise, but the words stopped,
smoked out and away, disheveled intent, and instead

I let you touch me again, deliberate, and in some stupor
agreed that the night could be colder, that we, too, could
burn longer if we leaned closer to the tree's rough bark.

We arrived identically with our backs pressed,
a confluence, and there was nothing in that bourbon bottle
that could lessen what I heard you say, your wooden horse
all at once the color of some midnight sun.

Sometimes, as we move closer to Autumn

Generosity weighs the pear boughs
down. Blooms this late in any season
are a warning. We have abandoned gathering
blossoms, but we carry their scent on our skin
from pressing our backs, shoulders, into their
ground nestings moments before these words,
left now, for you. We are involved in keeping

this tangling quiet, the way an inheritance
is expected by trees, through wind, swept
as sugar from hearth to threshold. I believe
in baptism the way the river carries convicts
and lovers both closer to something
like the sea. There is no end

to my hands covering your eyes. We
are fine lines carving the old rocks
and no tree here, no matter its sweetness,
its ripe remembering, can convince us
that the secret things are brighter
when we give them proper names.

This is how I answer goodnight

Gravity changes the way we say *Yes*.
Reclining means that I am relaxed enough
to tell you I could have drowned when you fell
asleep on the sand. I stood over your sun
bruised body, tiny crabs outlining your legs,
and collected my breath into lungs more
than burning, more than almost spent
completely. You did not wake then, not
for hours, and I let you burn a little,
watched your lips puff bright from simple
red to something like belladonna sheen.

I lie back, now, and admit that I never wanted you
to save me, that we save, each, ourselves, shells
already snug on our backs, curled smooth
as only skin pretending to be more than itself
can. I rest my head against your pillow and wait
for you to listen right, to see how far I've come
from undercurrent to woman who is asking you
not for forgiveness, but for knuckles to press
into shoulder blades, palms slow to fan,
when I roll to leave this space, yours, and walk
directly back into the ripe waiting sea.

Philosophy Tramples Everything, No Apologies

Let the fish suck at your finger. What you deduce
from the exchange of flesh-for-flesh will mean
throwing yourself, redemptive, at least in part,
into the river. We can love what's predatory
if we keep our bodies from being completely
swallowed. We can approach that cut wood
on fire, let ourselves and the thick rings sink
smoke first through skin to dirt, ripple water next.

This landscape is a finished painting before
your hand obscures the flock moving over
currents, connecting dots in an equation made
with wings beating faster than superstition, meaner
than our obligation to carve now from maybe tomorrow.
This is to say: one hand in mine, and one in the wet,
proves that it's hard to hold weapons while asking
for forgiveness. Today, there are pears in our basket
and though I do not know what to do with my mouth,
I can watch yours make sense of this story.

See? We are spies and often vain, yet undone
when, unchallenged, the other version
of each day ends likes this one: the fox breathing
underwater, the rabbit repeating what he hears,
and you and I a murmuration of lips circling
the overlapping body higher upward, upward.

This is the part where we don't say "love"

Tell me again how I'm sorry. Explain
how underneath your hands I am different
than when alone with my body. Make it up:
The long fence running from sandy yard to seaside.
Pretend to look out the window while you talk
to me. Show me what believing you means.
I cannot press against nowhere, or later.

Tell me how I want to be saved. In the backseat
of my car you called me *Princess* and I whispered
dragon and we almost sang.

This isn't the part where you remind me
that I sometimes ask for dirty things, windshield
muck thick ugliness. There is no mystery
in breaking twigs under my back when you push
hard into the cold grass, hips-against-hips.
This story is not that one.

When all the delineations point toward a happy ending,
tell me you know better. Say, we are both falling
from some bridge, but not really. Tell me how
we both jumped, waving our hands, tongues
out to the monsters we left long on the ground.

We name the totems with every morning

We say, *If I dive deep into the ocean*
and find a camel, everything I know
will cease to matter. This is how sleep
comes. We listen and turn dancer
tight into a curl against the bricks
resisting the bed's nightly push closer.

Let's pretend that the stories bind
our bodies. Promise that we never
expected familiarity, that when we like it
dirty, there is an opening waiting
to receive what we give to the maw.

We won't stay in out boxer shorts
even in the summer, not when someone
throws a shadow and reminds us nice
touch, when we begin to sing all the names
our histories remember, all the words
that make us comfortable on the side of this road.

Still talking about endings

Tell me how to roll-up and flee. When I touch
your wrist with three fingers and am checking
not for pulse but for birds, lilies, trapped, both
in their unfurling, under your skin, maybe
mine, tell me how to instead ache on my own.

Tonight you fill your mouth with pebbles
collected from our river's narrow bank
and this, too, is refusal to listen. How
can you hear the stories I surrender
with mica between your tooth and jaw?

Once there were two of us. And now
the briny pears are blossoming and every
walk I take without you is a reminder
that we left what matters spilt over silk
sheets we spread together to mark this and ours.

Imagine Not Drowning

Spiked edged milkweed and one morning
soon the ankle scrapes won't matter
and you will keep walking, pin dots
blooding-up your bones and shoes
right on past what was a minefield, bulbs
in orbit, neat circles and rows you planted
together. None of this means you are less
a dragon, less a waltzing wingman on fire.

Sometimes the leaving is not falling. Like this:
let's say you have discovered the feathered
starfish, unexpectedly waiting in its tidal pool
and you turn to say look, notice, again, aloneness
as heat escapes your skin and you are fine.

We sew-up the lies we keep inward, thread
colors as insignificant now as before. Hurl your body
up into the rain, head bent back, throat to the clouds.
You escape, you climb, and the crash you hear against
those rocks is not meant for confessions, not now. Kiss
your own fingers; you have carried yourself home.

Every Day We Devour the One Before

In the story, Raven
is devoured
by his own reflection.
In the telling,
seeds drop from your mouth
onto the stone
and we scurry, collecting
the white ones first,
black ones meant
for our pockets. What comes
next is irrelevant. It's no mystery
why we listen
only to ends and beginnings.
Have you noticed

that there are too many branches
for these birds? Have you seen
the distance between this wing's
tip and the buds refusing to open?

I woke up and asked
for endurance. You slept
and asked for nothing, darling,
your body shivering
as it does every morning
before you open
the box and let beaks
and bones predict
which of us sings along,
which uncovers the drum.

It's Only A Weapon When You Hold Your Breath

In the body, there is a better reason.
The belly, and the faithful spleen,
as if breathing, suggest that you are on fire,
in flames, the orange burning brighter
the longer you stay on your knees.

You could look up. You might show
the white flash of your throat, the way
it uncoils under the skin when you swallow.
This, too, means ash is not far behind.

What smolders changes the longer
you press your tongue to the tight roof
of that mouth, language unnecessary, coming
much later, in the rifle barrel night.

So, are you praying now, in that field
all concrete spidered weeds and week-
old daylight? There it is, that split between
kneeling and exile, middling the city's
open jaws and your own. It is easier to answer
with your head tilted back, lashes wet and black.

The Prettiness Is Up-Close

Now there is enough to enter
every name you have given
your father. No one is watching
and the day is more than over.

It's okay that you cannot collect
his urn. It's alright that you refuse
to drive from your apartment
to the funeral home (there is nothing
home in such a space) one more time.

Sometimes we are little more than torsos
in the dark. Our limbs deceive us, our heads
are not to be trusted from the moment
we close or open one or the other eye.

How, then, to hold the machete or the basket
carrying not just these oranges but every spice
and ribbon collected since the funeral,
where your mother's dress was not dark
enough and your shoulders were, as always, too pale?

There is no distance between tongue
and blade. There is no room wider
than the one wherein you wait, now,
to be told to dance, to strip it all
away and just roll from side to side
on the rough wood, tripwires balled tight.

You Say Disappear And I Say Not Yet

Seawater finds its way
from bucket back to sand
every time we fill, collect
what we might to build
something of our own
in a space that wants nothing
from us, not even our feet
wet and leaving.

Let's pretend we are just
wrong enough and our imprints
might stay where we place
them, totems, but bigger—more piss
than honey. We can cover our bodies
all day, say summer, draw-out unbreakable.

This is the closest thing we get
to surrender. It's draining, being
this vibrant, courting jealously
right out of the sky so the pelicans
glance down and drop their fat shining
fish right into our wide open maws.

There Are Ships Closer If You Let Them

You are kneeling on a quilt
printed with tiny jellyfish
their tentacles wrapping into pattern
after pattern. Your knees make a soft
well for softer bodies and suddenly
there are cotton currents beneath
bone and stretched skin.

If you will open your eyes
maybe you can rise, too, and leave
believing in the black bag getting heavy,
fat, with what you have made to be better,
to be motionless and good. I want

to tell you, your face pink, fevered just
so, that one morning, soon, I will take
you to the lighthouse you have painted.
I will take you to the rocks leading
upward where light rotates between fog
and whatever is left to love, to promise.

There is Enough Morning to Cleave the Skull From the Coral

What happens when we find the arrow nestled
in the lilies? Over the sand dune you see cresting
waves, taste brine when the tongue darts first
over flesh, next licks quick the soft hair wind
whipped across your lips. Will you bend, dipping
your waist inward to your navel, belling the back
into its own bow, meant for another archery altogether?

There is a grackle who reminds us that it is not yet
too late, but we ignore his song, speak louder to ourselves
about what we deserve, what we need. And you blame
some old lover for your forgetfulness. You tell me

about the woman whose spiral-inked hip is the leatherback
turtle's mark, flippers fading into grey into pink
into spaces your mouth refuses to forget. This is the story

you offer when I ask you to stop talking, to listen
to the men circling with their machetes, rum fisted,
pour ready, when a flash of white breast is all
the permission they need to come close enough
to fill my upturned palms, to plead with me, *beber, beber*

It's Only Running If You Refuse To Get Lost

Instead, I am still. Rather, the pebbles hit
the roof one at a time and I make no effort
to catch them on their way down to ping hard
metal, clay, collecting in rounding mounds
among broken glass bottles, nails
driven through shards, a barrier, a warning,
a symbol neither of us wants to name.

The cathedral is an unexpected intrusion. Christ,
His wounds permanently slick, lacquer bright,
his crown stationary, mine just won, still temple
cutting, pulling at errant hairs. We envy, together
the curls, nautilus tight, framing his face. Remember

how you told me to pack the largest spool
of copper wire, the coils not-quite red certain
to lead us, nearing night, back out of the salt-
fed forest? This steeple is also that one. The difference
is in the way you say look when we are facing first one
alter, stone and hibiscus, next the other, frond
and shells. I am luminous in all directions.

There are no wreaths hanging over the entrance
of this night's room; there are no reasons for finding
our way into the captain's graces, no matter how close
we run fingers, tips over spines, parallel to the plank.

Bravery, you said, is not what it used to be

Take atlases. We know they are drawn
by liars, that nowhere is set-- direction
only makes us brave the first time. So,
when you tell me that I cannot bend
the hand backward, I believe you
in the same way I have faith that benthos
are the only maps that make sense.

To make something simple
should be enough. When you say
"wrench," it isn't the object, the thing,
that sticks. Remember how you finger
my ribs, hilling the bones with tips, palming
each ridge down then up? Your head bends
next, tongue meeting my navel, hands occupying
another center entirely—this, too, is making.

The wrench belongs to the blessed boy
whose belly button nestled a golden
screw in its wrinkled cave. Consider how far
he traveled to ask a King's permission
for the tool to free the spiral knot
and loose for all and once whatever softness
might spill in the leaving. How many nights,
I ask you, did this boy sleep nearer wolves
than seagulls just to chance his own
inevitable unraveling? Consequences

are also simple. We break open our bellies,
leave the spine for licking clean, and as mapless
as we pretend to be, cannot risk surprise
when we fall, supplicant, to the ground.

Each of us a temple, a banquet lain over the cape

To all who eat without sense
to know better, to know
that consumption is reciprocal,
consider this a rapture. What we bring
inward is indecipherable, is code
for direction, maybe validation.
None of this matters when we sleep.

But tonight devastation is worn-
out, is worried away, and the mouth
is the edge of our river. Remember
Hera's catastrophe from breast
to milk to sky? She is like us:

The bosom asserts roundness
as our first fruit and we forget
the price of drinking a pathless
country into ever widening night.

There are shortcuts for burning the world

Let's say the man by the river loosens his bowtie.
From where we are sitting, the first silk paisley

is the thread, as it tumbles toward chest, from something
like want to causal woodpile leanings. Our throats know

tightness, too, and fingers find that liturgies are things
as much touched as heard. The triptych is this: glass

against rocks, calves passing the copperheads coiled
still, and our yawning wide into this late afternoon.

There are trout whose tails remind us that place
is a taproot mounding under both barn and cathedral.

Tell me when your shoulders become blackbirds. Say
we burn our fields before the first button exposes

the part of the neck meaning apple trees, asking
for nakedness in this current, laid down tenderly.

Unbreakable hour after hour

One more story from knees splintering
into the hardwood. Just another night
between July and not becoming
my mother's only child. So what
if the most beautiful part is the sucked-tight
rasp when he pulls back before in?

Are we listening; are we banished
yet? This is after I threw myself
into the well and swam, flew, clipped
the stone back up to open my throat
and say more. Crosshairs are one
thing when traced with tongue pointed
South. The trigger in my belly

is another. These are scarves
and fangs and radio dials lining
the ledge and I am still looking up
at you, your fingers nested in my fine hair,
and we both know what once upon time really means.

We replace the knives when the light appears

One morning, we don't remember the cost.
A joint widening its net polices the body
exactly twice: how your chest becomes
parenthetical to my spine and why
the breast cupped in your palm stays
bruised past breakfast. Outside, peonies
wait crushed into concrete and we are tanks

rolling them flatter, writing tiny scars
into headless snakes and red fur as words
you nail-dig into my arm, sometimes closing
my wrist to punctuate this ritual, this waking-
thirst as a basin aimed, open, catching
spunk thick wet. We depend on blurring
whose snout nuzzles the throat first.

Walking the lover past starlings' nests

Other people go to the planetarium. We stay
closer to gutter lines and concrete knowing damn
well what shines and where. In Kansas it's easier
to mark direction. Fields are like the mice they hide—
labyrinthine in morning, cosmos wide at night.

You and the horses talk late, emptying out demands
and apples in equal bundles, and there is no convincing
cadence between despair and those maps you make.

Every tortoise in a wild woman's cellar has a shell
you want to stroke. Sure, the pine throws a shadow.
Your back bent low to bring that jaw near a beak
casts shade that lasts just as long as bark growing
high for two thousand years. Look at us. Becoming

massive in the rooster's cocked open eye, his comb
tongue bright, a red remembered circling opals,
long after crinoline lay pooled by this bed, where now
we ask who climbs the tiny ladder first—who reaches
the carnival bag holding the fish won, the animal
we kept to populate, again, our backyard sea?

This is the center of disappear

There are only so many tickets given
in the background, and you slipping past,

collecting nothing, means another type
of looking away. You wear your body

as grief. Sometimes, you sleep too close
to an open window and moths lite

wherever your shoulder touched cotton.
Tell me who names the desert and watches

the Minotaur play with his paper ships
and I will savage the distance between

your weird breathing and my need
to have you, finally, again, inside. This

is never about affection. Ours is a recitation
billowing beyond generosity into artifact.

We come in anyway

I want to call you close to the window wood to listen
when the moth settles his antenna, alien fuzz
and vertices, against just fogged glass.

When the father asks if they want to die alone,
or be finished now, and quick, the men respond,
each in turn, in their long white rows, with a mouth
nicotine stained, then a head turned, slow to the right
or to the left—whichever way they remember
a window might face, though there are no breezes
and no songs here. We live everyday

with a child we do not know. Sometimes it is difficult
to understand whom is saving whom. The symptom
is sleep. Is it better to stay tucked into the blanket
we drape over the bed? Is it better to let the throat swell?

We hear sparrows in both winter and almost-spring. Why,
then, do we close the door every time a wing peeks
past our thresholds? You are the albino moose
who thinks about eating branches already
on the ground. Tell me what it means to begin
with anything, not knowing where it's going to go.

Quills are for the stories that stay written

We get lost, pirouette, and I count
the eggs, to be sure, tuck the basket
first under skirt, then decide instead
to balance the roundnesses, each,
on the hand's back. Every night

we do this: Love on water, a dragon
when you wish it, a harmony, three
parts, when you are tired. Tell me how

to swallow fronds, to let the bruised edges
hit the throat first, the virgin green staying
bright over lips covering, again, these teeth.

Let's pretend the princess leaves her mirror
in a bowl of cream. Sometimes the white
is the doe's tail when she leaps. Sometimes
the stomach is the clearing you circled
twice, and in this version, we both pull
our chins toward the clouds, drawing
the sky past the tree knot, past the need.

We make nothing from instinct

Let's pretend the old masters have given us four gifts.
How do we answer when the grandmother asks,
is it you, Ivan? We remember, at once, the feathers
don't come from the tail, they come from the breast.

The bosom belongs to women in both worlds, and to birds
whose intentions are to carry us only close to this or that edge.
Baba sets eleven heads on spikes. The twelfth, you recognize,
is empty. For you. Seeing such sharpness is the third gift.

We have met Viking ships after they pass under
low-bending birches. Every shore presses its forehead
closer to our cupped hands, filled as they are with brine,
the hard chests housing crabs collected beneath our feet.
The second gift we kept for ourselves, even though gulls
beg, wing-wounded, dim-witted and afraid.

In April, we pull our sticky bodies together, fitting
what's yours inside mine, and we forgot, entirely,
the lonely way shame obeys whomever reaches
the door, turns its knob enough to break ring and key.

The animal we love wags its tail even in the new dark

Listen to the way it has been told. This is how
we know those stories that begin before once
and sometimes during: We think to ourselves,
They are probably dancing in smoke and we
have been alone so long. Let us feast, let us
place the elk's skull over our eyes, too. What enters
the eyehole in this bone palace? When was the last

time you wore Hermes' helmet? Invisibility is every-
day. It's the accidental gifts that we trip over
on our way around the desert, the cacti blooming
hard. We endure rot because the music ants play
marks the first song we hear last. The problem
is the interval. The locus in the tension we tear
and tear while ignoring the leap we land, rooted
as we are in interiority. In the time before

time was stretched across that wooden rack,
we had a chance. Going down to the river
meant leaving the village behind only long enough
to mouth the songs, wet feet in a current, wrapping
arms and bows with arrows still strapped tight
against the back's two blades. Abundance

is gathering onions, meat dried through winter
and kept from Coyote. Sometimes we smell delicious
stew and before long we stand shoulder-to-tail
with every animal who never knew the leash.

How Far We Dive Is Only A Distraction

You are no one's father and a year
from now, when you walk into the clock-

maker's store and ask for whatever
he might be selling, your belly wounds

will reflect the petaling inward dance
you have practiced since falling first

from the oak, next from a trailer's steel
roof. You can't drown with a candle

lit in both hands. And I will see you leave,
small bag tucked near that elbow bent,

and if you turn toward my body, a climber
gathering honey in Nepal, bees halo-

wrapped again in summer, the ladder
will rope tight between us as it has

from village to cliff to stories we told
each other to pass night into one more morning.

If your chest to my spine is not quite enough

If not the fox, then the claw. This is how
you begin the first story, sticky flank-
to-flank after another night fucking, ocean
sounds not mechanized this time, the waking
to salt, finally real. I am listening, though thinking

of wildfires North, too far for either of us
to want a leaving, selfish distances not always
what they seem. It's simple and your neck
is still smeared with slick you left on my thigh
and I hear your voice say then she touched
the fur along its back and I consider swallowing,

again, the not-ready words. The old masters
may know all five appetites, but failing to tell
you even one means it's my turn to become a ladle
resting, steel mouth wide, in the well's water.

Seduction is the Lightening from this Season into Next

You cannot untwist the conversations
that point to why I love you. You think
She dances and there is a title in the movement
So I tell you, yes, write everything, but not
my name. Kicking at a stone does not lessen
how hard I see you, how when I lick my lips
I mean to say nothing else, to touch, instead
the space where your chest dips into stomach.

We are a belated topography. Your gestures
remind us both of the egg inside the egg inside
the tree, of the terrible, voluntary waiting.

I dedicate all my anguish, all my devastations
to whatever you might sing next. Just let me,
when you open your mouth, roundness, red,
be close enough to concede fully myself
to what beginning this might be, to what bird-
house we wriggle first one wing, then the next,
entirely into. Sing *vessel*, breathe *ours*.

Starch Coming First, Filling Hands Before Mouths Met Brine

When we leaned into the metal, snow
was already cleaved into grass, and stones
under tires were beginning to tumble pop
from worn black grooves onto tar. If you
unpocketed one hand, then the other, the reach
would be quick, and we both know that slowness
triggers falling. So, it's a minefield, beginning.

Extraordinary things gather when figs bloom
and the ripening is just torn from its season. We
are swept crumbles dusted quick into a pan, silver
handles from your thighs to mine. We might not
have names for hip bones in palms, but every-
day I carry the weight of your belt's brass
in the secret indentations leading, as a letter home,
to vestiges we might never speak to leave.

Seeing a Teeth Mother Mask, Together, On A Friday Afternoon

You see her clearly, call her Ecstatic
and Mother. There is hair, and there are beads,
and maybe no one else understands
why you cry when I tell you I have been
here before and named this woman
Terror, long before I took your arm
and whispered hush, told you her true name.

We walk, and I am pulling you along, a man
in love with being afraid, with, sometimes,
me. My father has died, and we talk, your words
occupying air, mine not quite joining, and the pendulum
swings hard when I ask you to tell me, promise
me that anger is temporal. Because you know. You
have been that speed increasing on the way down
and I have only just discovered evidence for such
velocity. Yet, the mask undoes you. So few

of us join hands and move sideways
around what we ought to bury. Now
we grow effortlessly up for having been,
somehow, reminded of reverse birthing. I know
what the teeth offer. You let us both pretend otherwise.

If the door notices you watching, it's only polite to look away

Touch me blurry, the way an ice cube distorts
smooth into gooseflesh on the way from clavicle
to areola. I'll give you the back of the book
and all my kitchen knives. I'll lay the objects
meant to obscure want close at your chest
while you wake, and, too, when you sleep. Just
slip the fingers in and pretend we found that cave
together, the one mouth-waiting past a rope-
bridge I made less from dreams than you know.

I am asking little. We are here, our hands cupping
the same brass handle, the same salted glass
touching our foreheads while rain forces
the sea that much nearer. Even when your teeth
scrape my back, I know the weight of you
is borrowed-- is the heron nodding past the bay.

Acknowledgments

Some of these poems appeared in a chapbook, *Some Animals*, published by *Etchings Press, Spring* 2016~

Some of theses poems appeared in a chapbook, *How We Disappear*, *Damfino Press*, Summer, 2016~

"*When He Leaves*" appeared in *2 Bridges Review*

"*Aphasia*" and "*How Much Tenderness*" appeared in *Linden Avenue*

"*Of Five Fears, three of them light.*" appeared in *Architrave*

"*Ghosting*" appeared in *The Boiler Journal*

"*Sorrow's Argument*" and "*What of Birds*" appeared in *TAB*

"*Eleven Years*" appeared in *Abridged*

"*We as Other People*" appeared in *Gravel*

"*If Fairy Tales in Fall*" appeared in *Modern Poetry Quarterly Review*

"*Edging Our Wall, Untying*", "*Deciding Against Marriage*", "*Some Animals*", "*Separations for Fall, for Winter, too*", and "*Folding the Invitation to Your Wedding*" all appeared in *The Inflectionist Review* (featured *Distinguished Poet* section)

"*Here Are Instructions for Removing the Scissors*" appeared in *East Bay Review*

"*Walking Through Morning*" appeared in *Pacifica*

"*Sometimes We Move Closer to Autumn*" appeared in *TOAD*

"*Reformation*" appeared in *Poetry Quarterly*

"*Market Day in Someone Else's City*" and "*Conversation Under Sun In Summer, Late*" appeared in *Lime Hawk*

"*This is How You ask me to Pray*" won the *2015 Pandora's Collective Poetry Prize*

"*Riding the borrowed cow back home*" appeared in *Restless*

"*When We Argue About Unraveling Glass*" appeared in *Blue Planet Journal*

"*Seeing a Teeth Mother Mask, Together, On A Friday Afternoon*" appeared in *Linden Avenue*

"*This is how you ask me to pray*" and "*Walking through the morning*" and "*Invitations toward Autumn*" appeared in *Two Thirds North*

"*Hushing Like and Awl Through Leather*" and "*When This is Not About Love*" appeared in *Rat's Ass Review*

"*Reformation*" appeared in *Poetry Quarterly*

"*Riding the borrowed cow back home*" appeared in *Wild Age Press*

"*How I answer goodnight*" and "*This is the part where we don't say love*" appeared in *TAB*

"*Imagine Not Drowning*" appeared as the *Editor's Choice* in *Panoply*

"*If the Door Notices*" and "*There is Enough Morning*" appeared in *Neck Press Review*

"*Starch Coming First*" appeared in *Red Fez*

"*The animal we love wags its tail even in the new dark*" appeared in *Bacopa Literary Review*

"*Walking the lover past the starlings*" and "*We Make Nothing From Instinct*" appeared in *Salt*

Thank You

A Note of Gratitude:

There is a scraggly yellow dog chasing his tail just across the road. Sometimes, I see him clearly and watch with an eye trained to look quickly away if he notices my stare.

In my pocket, I carry three keys, nine syllables, and seven words. In the writing of these poems, exactly one pirate and one crone have paid close attention to when my hand slips the pocket, and when the palm opens flat. I am grateful for both presences and why.

I am indebted to every reader, editor, and sassy corvid who have played with my poems and given the lines whatever attention they deserve. The sea, too, is owed thirteen fatty thank you's for refusing to drown me even when I swam too far, too often.

OTHER C&R PRESS TITLES

FICTION

Spectrum
by Martin Ott

That Man in Our Lives
by Xu Xi

A History of the Cat In Nine Chapters or Less
by Anis Shivani

SHORT FICTION

Notes From the Mother Tongue
by An Tran

The Protester Has Been Released
by Janet Sarbanes

ESSAY AND CREATIVE NONFICTION

While You Were Gone
by Sybil Baker

Je suis l'autre: Essays and Interrogations
by Kristina Marie Darling

Death of Art
by Chris Campanioni

POETRY

Collected Lies and Love Poems
by John Reed

Les Fauves
by Barbara Crooker

Tall as You are Tall Between Them
by Annie Christain

The Couple Who Fell to Earth
by Michelle Bitting

ANTHOLOGY

Zombies, Aliens, Cyborgs and the Ongoing Apocolypse
by Travis Denton and Katie Chaple

CHAPBOOKS

Notes from the Negro Side of the Moon
by Earl Braggs

A Hunger Called Music: A Verse History in Black Music
by Meredith Nnoka